DYNAMITE DINNERS

WAYLAND

First published in 2012 by Wayland

Copyright © Wayland 2012

Wayland
Hachette Children's Books
338 Euston Road
London NW1 3BR

Wayland Australia
Level 17/207 Kent Street
Sydney NSW 2000

Editor: Debbie Foy
Designer: Lisa Peacock
Photographer: Ian Garlick
Consultant: Sean Connolly
Proofreader/indexer: Sarah Doughty

British Library Cataloguing in Publication Data

Brash, Lorna.
Professor Cook's dynamite dinners.
1. Dinners and dining--Juvenile literature. 2. Entrees
(Cooking)--Juvenile literature. 3. Food--Composition--
Juvenile literature.
I. Title II. Dynamite dinners
641.5'4-dc23

ISBN: 978 0 7502 6852 3

Printed in China

Wayland is a division of Hachette Children's Books,
an Hachette UK Company.
www.hachette.co.uk

Contents

Professor Cook's Incredible Edibles 04

Sticky chicky burger stacks 06

Tex-Mex taco bowl salad 08

Incredible edible bowl soup! 10

Posh fish 'n' chips 'n' dip! 12

Pimp your burger! 14

Finger lickin' chicken satay 16

Japan-easy tuna rolls 18

Tongue-tingling sweet and sour noodles 20

Thirsty couscous cakes! 22

Scrambly egg fried rice 24

Superfood cannelloni 26

Chilli with a deep, dark secret 28

Professor Cook's glossary 30

Index & useful websites 32

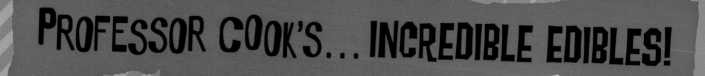

PROFESSOR COOK'S... INCREDIBLE EDIBLES!

ARE you hungry to LEARN MORE about your food?

Have you ever wondered why some foods behave the way they do? For example, have you ever wondered how delicious Chinese noodles can taste sweet and sour at the same time? Or have you ever added avocado to your salad and noticed that it turned from green to brown almost immediately?

Well, join Professor Cook and his team to find out the answers to these and many more questions about some of the fascinating ways that our food behaves. Find out what makes a superfood so super, how to make a soup bowl that you can REALLY eat and find out the deep, dark secret to cooking an amazing chilli!

HAPPY ~~EXPERIMENTING~~ COOKING!

PROFESSOR COOK'S KITCHEN RULE BOOK

→ Always wash your hands before you start cooking and after handling raw meat

→ Mop up spills as soon as they happen

→ Use oven gloves for handling hot dishes straight from the oven

→ Take care with sharp knives. Don't walk around with them!

→ Switch off the oven or cooker top when you have finished cooking

→ Use separate chopping boards for vegetables and meat

→ Store raw and cooked foods separately in the fridge

→ Don't forget to tidy up the kitchen afterwards! No brainer, huh?

HOT GOODS!

WHEN YOU SEE THIS WARNING SIGN AN ADULT'S HELP MAY BE NEEDED!

The 'Science Bits'

Believe it or not, cooking involves a lot of science! The Science Bits that accompany each of Professor Cook's delicious recipes answer all the mysteries about food that you have ever wondered about. They also explore some of the interesting, unusual or downright quirky ways that our food can often behave!

STICKY CHICKY BURGER STACKS

Everybody loves a burger! And good, wholesome burgers are made from good quality minced meat. But what is it that gives the burger its shape and what stops it from falling apart on your barbecue or grill? Read on...

Step 1

In a large bowl mix together the minced chicken, soy sauce, chilli dipping sauce, lemon rind and juice and spring onions. Season with salt and freshly ground black pepper. Next, get your hands into the mixture and give it a good squeeze until all the ingredients are thoroughly combined.

Step 2

Divide the mixture into 8 equal-sized balls, then flatten them slightly so that you have 8 mini burgers. Place on a baking tray lined with foil.

Step 3

Preheat the grill to hot. Cook the burgers under the grill for 7-8 minutes on each side until cooked through. While the burgers are cooking, split the rolls and tear the lettuce leaves in half. Place one torn lettuce leaf over 8 halves of the rolls. Top with the sliced tomatoes. Place the cooked burgers over the top then add the bread roll lids. Serve with homemade mayonnaise or ketchup (page 14-15).

The Science Bit

What holds your burger together?

The stuff that stops your burger (as well as people and most animals!) falling apart is a protein called collagen. Minced meat contains collagen and when it is cooked with a liquid (in this case soy sauce) the collagen is broken down into a softer substance called gelatine (used to make jelly!).

This binds the minced meat together and helps your burger to keep its yummy, burger-y shape!

The Science Bit

Why does peeled avocado quickly turn brown?

Avocados (and lots of other fruits) turn brown when exposed to air because of a chemical reaction known as oxidation. But we can help to stop this reaction with a squeeze of lemon juice! Why? Because vitamin C in the lemon juice (called ascorbic acid) slows down the oxidation process and helps the avocado to stay fresh and green for longer!

Stuff you need:

4 large soft flour tortillas
2 tbsp olive oil
1 little gem lettuce
100g cherry tomatoes, halved
1/4 cucumber, finely chopped
400g tinned mixed bean salad, drained
200g sweetcorn kernels
1 avocado, cut into chunks and tossed with 2 tbsp lemon juice
4 tbsp vinaigrette dressing
50g Cheddar cheese, grated

Serves 4

Avocados have the highest protein content of any fruit!

TEX-MEX TACO BOWL SALAD

Make your own edible taco bowl to serve this delicious salad! Work quickly with the avocado to keep it looking fresh and green - add it at the end and serve immediately.

Step 1

Preheat the oven to 180°C/fan 160°C/gas mark 4. Brush the tortillas with oil on both sides and place in heatproof bowls, shaping the sides to make a 'taco bowl'. Bake for 8-9 minutes until crisp and set into a bowl shape. Allow the taco bowls to cool completely before removing.

Step 2

Shred the lettuce and toss with the tomatoes, cucumber, beans, sweetcorn, avocado with lemon juice and dressing. Spoon the salad into the taco bowls.

Step 3

Finally, scatter the grated cheese over the top and serve!

INCREDIBLE EDIBLE BOWL SOUP!

Here's an amazing fish soup which allows you to eat the bowl AND its contents! And while we're at it, let's have a look at how the haddock gets its lovely smoky flavour...

Stuff you need:

6 crusty cob bread rolls
1-2 tbsp olive oil
500g potatoes, peeled
1 large onion, peeled
1.2 litres milk
1 garlic clove, crushed
300g tinned sweetcorn with red pepper, drained
450g smoked haddock fillets, skinned
Salt and black pepper
Handful flat-leaf parsley, chopped

Serves 6

Step 1

Preheat the oven to 200°C/fan 180°C /gas mark 6. Pinch a 'lid' from the top of the bread roll and set aside. Then scoop out the soft bread from inside leaving a ½-inch layer of bread inside.

When you toast a slice of bread a chemical reaction occurs that alters the sugars and proteins in the bread!

Step 2

Brush the insides of the rolls with oil and bake for 15 minutes until golden. This will 'seal' the inside of the roll. Chop the potatoes and onion into small chunks and place in a large saucepan.

Step 3

Add the milk to the potatoes and onion and bring to the boil. Turn down the heat, cover and simmer for 10 minutes.

Step 4

Next, stir in the garlic, sweetcorn mixture and fish. Bring back to the boil, then turn down the heat, cover and simmer for 5 minutes until the fish flakes easily with a fork. Season to taste with salt and pepper. Stir in the parsley.

Step 5

Spoon the soup into the bread rolls and serve (and eat!) immediately.

The Science Bit

Why do we smoke fish?

Before fridges were invented freshly caught fish was preserved by smoking it over slow burning wood chips to stop it from rotting. Smoking absorbs moisture from the fish and inhibits the growth of bacteria which can cause it to decay. Smoking also stops fat on the surface of the fish 'going off' (due to oxidation), and so protects the inside of the fish, which is good to eat!

POSH FISH 'N' CHIPS 'N' DIP!

A fish and chip supper is a yummy treat – and one that might even help to make you a bit brainier...!

Step 1

Preheat the oven to 200°C/fan 180°C/gas mark 6. Cut the potatoes lengthways into wedges and toss with the olive oil. Spread into a single layer on a baking sheet, sprinkle with salt and pepper and roast for 30–35 minutes until crisp and golden.

Step 2

To make the dip, finely chop the watercress and stir into the mayonnaise. Add the gherkins. Chill until ready to use.

Stuff you need:

2 large baking potatoes
1 tbsp olive oil
Rock salt and ground black pepper
Small handful watercress
6 tbsp mayonnaise
4 baby gherkins, finely chopped
50g plain flour
2 large eggs, beaten
100g fresh ciabatta breadcrumbs
1/4 tsp cayenne pepper
650g skinned haddock, cod or salmon fillets, cut into strips
4 tbsp sunflower oil, for shallow frying

Serves 4

HOT GOODS!

Step 3

Place the flour, the eggs and the breadcrumbs (mixed with the cayenne pepper) into three separate dishes. First, dip the fish into the flour to coat, then into the egg and finally into the breadcrumbs to coat evenly.

Step 4

Pour about 2cm of oil into a deep frying pan and heat until a piece of bread turns golden in 30 seconds. Cook the fish in batches for 2-3 minutes until crisp and golden. Drain on kitchen paper and keep warm while cooking the remaining fish. Serve hot with the chips and the gherkin mayo dip.

The Science Bit

Does eating fish really make you brainy?

You've heard this loads of times, right? Well, while eating fish won't instantly make your maths homework easier, scientists believe there is some truth to it. The 'magic' ingredient in fish is omega-3 fatty acids which are found in all fish but mainly in 'oily' fish such as fresh tuna, mackerel, sardines, herring and salmon!

PIMP YOUR BURGER!

Ketchup-at-home

What's thick and red and great with chips? Yep, it's tomato ketchup. Make your own super homemade version to serve with Sticky Chicky Burger Stacks (page 6).

Step 1

Place all the ingredients except the sugar into a food processor and whizz to a smooth puree.

Step 2

Pour the puree into a pan and bring to the boil. Sprinkle over the sugar and stir until dissolved. Reduce the heat and simmer for 30 minutes, stirring until thickened. Allow to cool for 5-10 minutes.

Step 3

Decant the ketchup into a clean container. Seal and store in the fridge. Use within 3 weeks once opened.

Stuff you need:

400g tomato puree
225ml cider vinegar
2 onions, peeled and finely chopped
1 large potato, peeled and diced
50g fresh root ginger, peeled and finely grated
2 sticks celery, finely chopped
3 garlic cloves, crushed
1 tsp ground cinnamon
1 tsp ground cloves
2 tsp fine table salt
1 tsp freshly ground black pepper
125g muscovado sugar

Makes 600ml

HomEMAdE MAyo

Q:How do two liquids combine together to make a yummy, thick and creamy mayonnaise?
A:See 'The Science Bit' for an explanantion of this kitchen magic!

Step 1

Whisk the egg yolks, salt, mustard and vinegar with an electric whisk until well combined. Add the oil a spoonful at a time and whisk until the mixture starts to thicken. Continue until all of the oil has been used.

Step 2

Flavour up your mayo with 1–2 tbsp barbecue sauce, tomato ketchup or a small handful of chopped herbs, spring onions or chives.

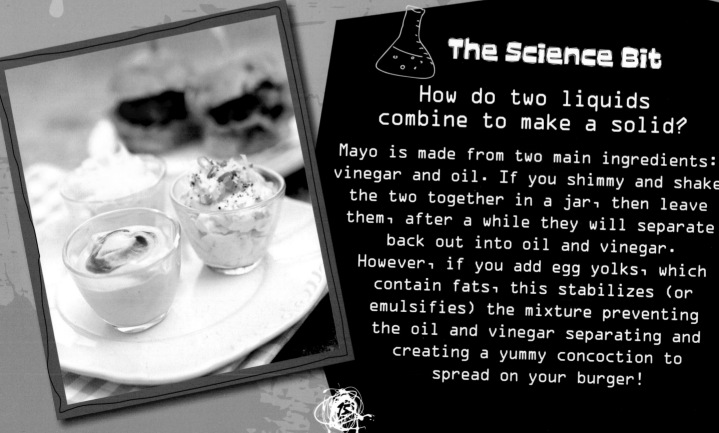

The Science Bit

How do two liquids combine to make a solid?

Mayo is made from two main ingredients: vinegar and oil. If you shimmy and shake the two together in a jar, then leave them, after a while they will separate back out into oil and vinegar. However, if you add egg yolks, which contain fats, this stabilizes (or emulsifies) the mixture preventing the oil and vinegar separating and creating a yummy concoction to spread on your burger!

FINGER LICKIN' CHICKEN SATAY

You'll be licking your lips as well as your fingers with these marinated chicken sticks dipped in a perfectly peanutty sauce. It's a promise!

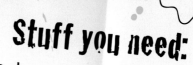

Stuff you need:

12 bamboo skewers
500g boneless skinless chicken breasts
4 tbsp soy sauce
1 tbsp runny honey
1 tsp minced ginger
1 tsp minced garlic
Small handful fresh chopped coriander
4 tbsp crunchy peanut butter
3 tbsp sweet chilli dipping sauce
Lemon wedges, to serve

Makes 12 skewers

Step 1

Place the bamboo skewers in a shallow dish and spread them into a single layer. Pour cold water over them to cover. Leave for at least 30 minutes to soak.

Kitchen alert! Wash your hands after handling raw chicken

Step 2

Cut the chicken into chunks and place in a bowl with 2 tbsp of the soy sauce, honey, minced ginger, garlic and coriander. Give all the ingredients a good mix. Cover and set aside for 30 minutes.

Step 3

Remove the skewers from the water. Thread the chicken pieces onto the skewers and place on a baking tray. Cook them under a hot grill for 4-5 minutes on each side until golden brown.

Step 4

Place the peanut butter, remaining soy sauce, sweet chilli sauce and 90ml water into a saucepan and heat gently until smooth and thick. Serve the satay sticks with the peanut sauce and a squeeze of fresh lemon.

The Science Bit

Can I make healthier peanut butter at home?

Yes you can! Just whizz up 500g unsalted shelled peanuts, 2 tbsp peanut oil and a pinch of salt in a food processor. Keep it in a sealed container in the fridge and use within two weeks. The homemade stuff avoids using sweeteners and preservatives which help to prolong the shelf life of shop-bought peanut butter. Overall, your homemade version is much healthier!

JAPAN-EASY TUNA ROLLS

Made with one of the staple ingredients of Japanese food, sticky white rice, these sushi rolls are easy to eat – even with chopsticks!

Step 1

Wash the rice under the cold tap until the water runs clear. Place into a saucepan and add 475ml cold water. Bring the rice to the boil, then cover, reduce the heat and simmer for 15 minutes. Do NOT lift the lid. Leave the rice to stand for 10 minutes, then stir in the rice vinegar.

Step 2

Place a piece of clingfilm a little larger than the nori sheet onto a work surface. Place the nori sheet on top. Spoon a third of the cooked rice into the centre of the nori sheet and spread to the edges leaving a 2-cm space along one edge of the nori.

18

Step 3

Mix the tuna and mayo and spread a third of it across the centre of the rice. Arrange a third of the pimento and cucumber sticks along the centre of the tuna mixture.

Step 4

Use the clingfilm to help you roll up the nori. The uncovered strip of nori will make a good 'seal' to the end of your sushi roll. Repeat with the remaining ingredients to make two more rolls.

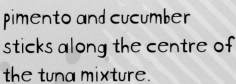

Step 5

Unwrap the rolls and cut each into 5 equal-sized pieces. Dip your sushi pieces into soy sauce, eat and enjoy!

The Science Bit

Why is sushi rice so super-sticky?

It's the starch in rice that makes it so sticky. When you cook this short-grain rice, the water and heat soak into the grain and the starch molecules break down and absorb water to form a sticky 'gel' (this process is called gelatinization). Sushi rice is cooked using the absorption method which means no water remains after cooking. So the starch released into the water is then readily gobbled back up by the rice grain making it super-sticky!

Wow! Rice husks are so tough that in some countries they are used to make concrete!

19

TONGUE-TINGLING SWEET AND SOUR NOODLES

Get your taste buds a-jangling with this noodle dish that combines a range of flavours to really tantalize your tongue!

Step 1

Heat the oil in a wok or large frying pan and fry the onion for 3–4 minutes. Stir in the garlic, mushrooms, red pepper and carrot and stir-fry for 3 minutes more.

Stuff you need:

1 tbsp sunflower oil
1 small onion, chopped
1 garlic clove, crushed
140g button mushrooms, sliced
1 red pepper, deseeded and thinly sliced
1 carrot, peeled and cut into sticks
227g tin pineapple chunks in natural juice
1 tbsp cornflour
Juice of 1 lemon
2 tbsp tomato puree
3 tbsp soy sauce
125g egg noodles
2 spring onions, trimmed and sliced

Serves 4

Step 2

Drain the pineapple chunks reserving the juice in a measuring jug. Add enough cold water to the pineapple juice to make 200ml of liquid. Add the pineapple to the stir-fry mixture and cook for 2–3 minutes, stirring occasionally.

Step 3

Meanwhile, mix the cornflour with the lemon juice to form a smooth white paste. Stir in the tomato puree, soy sauce and pineapple juice liquid.

Step 4

Cook the noodles in a pan of lightly salted boiling water according to the packet instructions. This should take about 3-4 minutes.

Step 5

Add the noodles to the stir-fry mixture and pour over the sauce. Turn up the heat and cook for 1-2 minutes, stirring until the sauce has become thick and glossy, coating all the ingredients. Scatter with the onions, then eat with chopsticks if you can!

 ## The Science Bit

Can you taste sweet <u>and</u> sour?

Your tongue is covered with tiny little taste sensors called papillae. These detect the molecules in your food that gives it flavour. Scientists believe that we can detect five different flavours with our papillae. These are sweet, sour, salt, bitter and umami, which is a highly savoury, meaty flavour found in such foods as tomatoes and cured meat.

THIRSTY COUSCOUS CAKES!

Couscous is a North African food that is traditionally steamed and served with rich stews. The tiny couscous granules soak up boiling water as if by magic!

Stuff you need:

50g couscous
Large handful fresh coriander, finely chopped
1 small garlic clove, crushed
3 tbsp olive oil
1/2 tsp ground cumin
1/2 tsp ground coriander
2 tbsp pine nuts, toasted
50g feta cheese, finely diced
2 medium eggs, beaten
150g fine white breadcrumbs
Salt and black pepper
2 tbsp plain flour
4 tbsp sunflower oil, for shallow frying

Serves 4

HOT GOODS!

Step 1

Place the couscous in a large bowl and cover with 100ml of boiling water. Leave to stand for 10 minutes, then fluff up with a fork.

Step 2

Place the fresh coriander, garlic, oil, cumin and ground coriander into a food processor and whizz to a thick puree. Stir into the couscous with the pine nuts, feta cheese, half the beaten egg and half the breadcrumbs until well combined. Season with salt and pepper. Roll into 8 small balls and then flatten into burger shapes.

Step 3

Put the flour, the remaining egg and the remaining breadcrumbs into separate dishes (as shown). Dip the couscous cakes into the flour to cover, then into the beaten egg and finally the breadcrumbs to coat.

Step 4

Heat the oil in a frying pan. Carefully cook the couscous cakes in batches for 3 minutes on each side until golden. Serve with salad and homemade mayonnaise (see page 15).

The Science Bit

Why does couscous grow?

Couscous is granules of semolina made from durum wheat (the same stuff that pasta is made from). Durum wheat is high in gluten, a type of protein. The Latin word gluten means 'glue', and that gives us a clue as to why couscous grows, as it attracts and absorbs liquids. When you pour boiling water over the couscous, each granule can absorb its own volume in water, which makes it double in size!

23

SCRAMBLY EGG FRIED RICE

This is a totally dynamite dinner recipe that you can make so quickly and easily! Apart from the juicy chicken and vegetables, the little egg-coated grains of rice are what makes it oh-so special. So, come on, eggs – tell us how you do it!

Stuff you need:

350g long-grain rice
2 tbsp groundnut oil
2 garlic cloves, crushed
450g skinless chicken breasts, chopped
1 red pepper, deseeded and chopped
1 tbsp curry powder
1 bunch spring onions, thinly sliced
75g frozen peas, defrosted
2 tbsp light soy sauce
2 eggs, lightly whisked
Small handful fresh coriander, chopped

Serves 4

HOT GOODS!

The Science Bit

Why do eggs scramble?

Egg is a protein which changes instantly when heat is added. Proteins are made up of long chains of amino acids. When you whisk the white and yolk of an egg together you are creating new chemical bonds between the proteins in the egg white and the proteins in the yolk. Water from the yolk is trapped along with air, which was added when you whisked the eggs. Once heat is added the proteins clump together. If unstirred they form an omelette, but if stirred they form scrambled eggs as you are breaking down the protein connections.

26

Step 1

Bring a large pan of lightly salted water to the boil. Add the rice and stir with a wooden spoon. Cook for 12-15 minutes. Carefully lift the saucepan and pour the rice into a sieve.

Step 2

Pour the oil into a deep frying pan or wok. Heat gently then add the garlic, chicken and pepper and stir-fry for 8-10 minutes. Add the curry powder and cook for 1 minute.

Step 3

Add the cooked rice, spring onions and peas and cook for 5 minutes, stirring occasionally to make sure the ingredients do not stick. Drizzle over the soy sauce.

Step 4

Push the rice mixture to one side of the pan. Pour the eggs into the uncovered part and stir until they scramble, then mix with the rice. Scatter with coriander and serve!

SUPERFOOD CANNELLONI

Bright green spinach is a superhero's staple food as it's jam-packed to the brim with vitamins A and C, plus iron, zinc and potassium. Go get some on your plate!

Stuff you need:

800g baby spinach leaves
Freshly grated nutmeg
6 sheets fresh lasagne
450g low-fat cream cheese
2 tbsp olive oil
1 large onion, peeled and finely chopped
2 garlic cloves, crushed
1 red pepper, deseeded and chopped
400g tinned chopped tomatoes
1 tbsp tomato puree
2 tsp dried Italian herbs
400ml passata
100ml vegetable stock
Salt and black pepper
50g grated mozzarella cheese
Basil leaves

Serves 4-6

Step 1

Rinse the spinach well and place in a large saucepan. Heat gently, stirring, until the spinach starts to wilt. Sieve out any excess liquid, then add a pinch of nutmeg.

Step 2

Lay the lasagne sheets out on a work surface and spread with the cream cheese to cover. Lay the wilted spinach over the cream cheese.

Step 3

Roll up the lasagne sheets from the short end and place in a large ovenproof dish (large enough so that the lasagne rolls are in a single layer).

Step 4

Preheat the oven to 180°C/fan 160°C/gas mark 4. Heat the oil in a large saucepan and fry the onion, garlic and red pepper until softened. Stir in the tomatoes, tomato puree, herbs, passata and stock. Bring to the boil, cover and simmer for 20 minutes.

Step 5

Season with salt and pepper and then pour over the cannelloni rolls. Scatter over the cheese and bake for 30 minutes until bubbling. Garnish with basil leaves and serve with lots of green salad.

The Science Bit

Why is spinach so good for you?

Spinach is known as a superfood. It is low in calories and packed full of vitamins and minerals. To improve our body's absorption of iron from the spinach, it should be eaten with a source of vitamin C. So, squeeze fresh lemon juice onto cooked spinach before you eat it, or eat your superfood cannelloni with a large glass of fresh orange juice!

Stuff you need:

2 tbsp sunflower oil
500g lean minced beef
2 large onions, peeled and chopped
2 garlic cloves, crushed
1 tsp each ground cumin, coriander and oregano
1 tbsp mild chilli powder
1 red pepper, deseeded and chopped
125g chestnut mushrooms, sliced
2x 400g tins kidney beans, drained
2x 400g tins chopped tomatoes
2 tbsp tomato puree
2 tsp Worcestershire sauce
25g dark plain chocolate, finely chopped
Salt and black pepper

Serves 6

The Science Bit

Chillies and chocolate?

You may think the idea of putting chocolate and chillies together a bit weird, but the Mexicans have long since added chocolate to their 'mole' (sauces). As a fresh red chilli dries it develops a sweet, fruity flavour which, when combined with chocolate, makes an awesome combination. It is also thought that the richness of the melted chocolate helps to tone down some of the heat from the chilli.

CHILLI WITH A DEEP, DARK SECRET

A big hurrah for chilli – served with jacket potato, fluffy rice or any which way. But do you know the secret ingredient that Mexicans add to make the sauce truly rich and creamy?

Step 1

Heat the oil in a large pan and fry the minced beef for 5-6 minutes, stirring occasionally until browned all over.

Step 2

Add the onions and garlic and stir well. Cook for 3-4 minutes stirring now and then. Add the cumin, coriander, oregano and chilli powder and cook for 1-2 minutes. Don't allow the mixture to stick to the bottom of the pan.

Step 3

Add the remaining ingredients and bring to the boil. Season with salt and pepper. Cover and simmer gently for 45 minutes, stirring occasionally. Serve with rice or jacket potato.

AMINO ACIDS these molecules are the building blocks of protein

BACTERIA tiny living organisms that can grow on food

BAMBOO SKEWERS wooden sticks on which you can thread meat, fish or vegetables for grilling or barbecuing

CALORIES units of energy that are contained within the food you eat

COLLAGEN a protein found in animal tissue. When heated collagen turns to gelatine

CORNFLOUR a white powder that is used to thicken liquids such as soups, stews and gravies

EDIBLE something (usually a food substance) that we can eat

ELECTRIC HAND WHISK a hand-held mixer with two or three whisks attached

EMULSIFY to add a substance that stabilizes a mixture, for example adding an egg yolk to oil and vinegar and stops them from separating out. This process is known as emulsification

FRY to cook with oil in a shallow frying pan

GELATINE a setting agent used in many puddings and desserts

MINERALS substances in food that help your body grow, develop and stay healthy

NORI dried sheets of seaweed used in making sushi rolls

OMEGA-3 FATTY ACIDS found mainly in oily fish, these are essential for growth, brain function and the nervous system

OXIDATION the reaction that occurs when a food substance is exposed to air

PIMENTO a large red pepper, which is generally chargrilled, skinned and bottled or canned in brine (salt water)

POTASSIUM a mineral found in foods such as avocados, dried apricots, white beans, fish and dates and which is essential in maintaining the nervous system

PRESERVATIVES substances added to food to prevent it from spoiling

SEASON to flavour food with salt and pepper

SIEVING to drain ingredients through a sieve to remove the water

SOLID something that is firm and keeps its shape, compared to a liquid which has to be contained

SUPERFOODS nutrient-rich foods that fight off ageing and illness. Packed full of vitamins, minerals and antioxidants, these help the cells in our bodies grow, reproduce and repair

TOSS to lightly throw ingredients (usually salads) together to properly combine them

WHISK to beat with a light, rapid motion

WOK a large, deep frying pan used in Chinese cooking

INDEX

amino acids 24
avocados 4, 8, 9

bacteria 11
bread 6, 7, 10, 11
burgers 6, 7

calories 27
cannelloni 26, 27
chillies 28
chocolate 28
chopping boards 5
collagen 7
couscous 22, 23

eggs 15, 24, 25
emusifier 15

fish and chips 12, 13
flavours 21
fridges 5, 11

gelatine 7

hygiene 5

iron 26, 27

ketchup 14, 15
kitchen rules 5
knives 5

mayonnaise 12, 13, 15, 23
meat, raw 5, 16
minerals 27

noodles 4, 20, 21

omega-3 fatty acids 13
oven gloves 5
oven safety 5
oxidation 8

peanut butter 16,17
potassium 26
preservatives 17
protein 8, 10, 24

rice 18, 19, 24, 25

smoking foods 10, 11
solids 15
soup 10, 11
spills 5
spinach 26, 27
starch 19
superfoods 4, 27
sushi rolls 18, 19
sweet and sour 4, 20, 21
sweeteners 17

taste sensors 21
toasting 10

vitamins 8, 26, 27

wheat 23
wok 20, 25

zinc 26

USEFUL WEBSITES

www.spatulatta.com
Get some basic cooking skills under your belt, with step-by-step video recipes and a recipe box that includes options for cooking a meal by choosing a basic ingredient, a type of food, occasion or particular diet.

www.yummyscience.co.uk
Super-fun science projects to try out in the kitchen using everyday foods. Grow your own crystals with salt, test out the toasting properties of bread or make your own honeycomb toffee. Some of these recipes call for an adult's help, so always make sure you let an adult know before you start.

www.exploratorium.edu/cooking
Find out how a pinch of curiosity can improve your cooking! Explore recipes, activities and webcasts that will improve your understanding of the science behind food and cooking.

Discover some more incredible edibles with PROFESSOR COOK and the team!

Smashing Snacks

9780750268516

Pop-tastic popcorn
Smashing caramel shards
Ice cream in a bag
Cheese-and-ham-o-rama!
Homemade beans on toast
Oat-so yummy power cookies
'No-cry' onion bhajis
Double-dipped mallow cookies
Mini superhero pies!
Gold bullion honeycomb bars!
Pink fizz-bomb lemonade
Big dipper breadsticks
Professor Cook's glossary
Index

Mind-Blowing Bakes

9780750268837

Oozing crust pizza
Stack 'em high cheesy puff pie
Exploding cupcakes
Stained glass cookies
Crimson velvet whoopie pies!
Very berry choco meringues
Kitchen sink pot pies
Hot ice cream sparkle
Super seedy flowerpot bread
Choc pops
Black and blue buns
Squidy widgy custard tarts
Professor Cook's glossary
Index

Dynamite Dinners

9780750268523

Sticky chicky burger stacks
Tex Mex taco salad bowl
Incredible edible bowl soup!
Posh fish 'n' chips 'n' dip!
Pimp your burger!
Finger lickin' chicken satay
Japan-easy tuna rolls
Tongue-tingling sweet and sour noodles
Thirsty couscous cakes!
Scrambly egg fried rice
Superfood cannelloni
Chilli with a deep, dark secret
Professor Cook's glossary
Index

Fascinating Fruits

9780750268844

Tropical fruit with goo-ey chocolate dip
Incredible edible tie-dye lollies
Icy watermelon slices
Hot caramelised pineapple lollies
Super blueberry cheesecake
Homemade yoghurt with fruit squish
'Magic' apple and blackberry pudding
Nicey slicey summer fruit jelly
Wobbly strawberry mousse
Ice bowl fruit salad
Instant frozen yoghurt
Sticky licky banoffee cones
Professor Cook's glossary
Index

WAYLAND